History of Japan

From early history
to the present day

by Viktoria Niebuhr

Table of Contents

Introduction

Marco Polo was the first to mention the Japanese territory of Eastern Asia around 1300 in his writings. Zipango (the medieval name for Japan in Europe) was in his mind a land covered with gold, silver and pearls. This and many other mysteries persisted until the first actual arrival of globetrotters from Europe. Japan was a distant beauty to explore.

Today, Japan likes to present itself to the public as a unit. However, the complexity of its culture can quickly be guessed if one considers the geographically extensive area (377,835 km²) on which the country stretches. Differences in religion, language and cuisine are therefore indispensable. The different climate zones that Japan encompasses also contribute to the country's diversity.

Japan is a fertile country. It consists of vast mountain landscapes, many waters and unique flora and fauna. The four main islands Hokkaido, Shinkoku, Kyushu and Honshu together form the national territory. The largest island Honshu is home to approx. 80 per cent of the total population, and represents the economically strongest area of Japan, among other things because of the Tokyo/Kanto region.

Hunted down by numerous volcanic eruptions, tsunamis and earthquakes, Japan is a country that must be prepared for disasters. This was demonstrated by the nuclear disaster in Fukushima (2011). The reason for this is the four tectonic plates that unite Japan. An insanely frequented quake, which fortunately goes unnoticed most of the time, is on the Japanese agenda due to this geographical localization. Sometimes, strengths of up to nine on the Richter scale can be achieved, of which the population can be warned early enough due to advanced technology. The Japanese house construction method has adapted to the geographical conditions and therefore offers good stability. In addition, Japanese citizens became aware of how to behave in emergency situations early on.

Japan is located in the so-called "Pacific Ring of Fire", a geographical belt consisting of volcanoes. This surrounds the Pacific from three sides. Since most of Japan has a deep-sea coast, the danger of tsunamis is drastically increased. The large urban agglomerations around Tokyo are due to this narrow settlement area.

Japanese time counting begins with the Kofun period (ca. 300 - 552 AD). Japan corresponded closely with its neighbours, China and Korea. The empire came into being. However, the country's early history also reflects important events that underpin Japanese cultural understanding. Here, it is important to distinguish between mythological and factually proven traditions. There are different research results based on different sources and dates.

The following text provides an introduction to the current scientific consensus in Japanese history. The different epochs, from early history to modern times, are examined for their peculiarities and their explosiveness with regard to the development of Japan. Furthermore, the text examines the effects of history on Japanese social and economic structures. Today's Japan is the last topic of this introduction. Finally, we look at the future of Japan, with possible problems arising from the present.

Early History (about 30.000 years ago until 300 A.D.)

Jomon-Period

The history of Japan began with Stone Age people who arrived on the Japanese archipelagos some 30,000 years ago. Before the Ice Age, the approximately 8,500 islands could still be reached by humans via existing connections to the mainland. This changed with the rise of the sea level, which brought Japan into the geographically isolated position that still exists today. The Stone Age civilization, which began with the end of the last ice age is called Jomon culture.

The primitive people of the Ainu only began to fully inhabit Japan 15,000 years after the Stone Age. The Mongols from Central Asia followed. At first, there was a peaceful coexistence of both peoples. The spread of famines became a problem for the Ainu, who were largely displaced from their habitat by the Mongols, and conflicts arose between the two ethnic groups.

The Ainu anchored their religious rites in their belief in nature. The first beginnings of an archetype of Shintoism can be seen here since the Ainu worshipped a plurality of different deities, the so-called "Kamuy". Elements such as fire and water, but also weather forces such as lightning and thunder, were attributed to a god, as were animals and plants. The spirituality of this people was accompanied by a great respect for nature. According to the Ainu faith, the gods protected mountains, forests and waters.

The people of young Japan lived largely cut off from the outside world. They kept themselves afloat as collectors, hunters and fishermen. They also practiced pottery, which today bears the name of Jomon ceramics. The name "Jomon" means "cord print decoration" (Jomon). The typical, flame-like patterns of this ceramic were created by pressing a string on the surface of the still malleable clay.

Yayoi period (300 B.C. - 300 A.D.)

In 300 B.C., the first Korean immigrants flocked into the country. They brought rice cultivation and other agriculture, as well as horses and cattle to Japan for the first time.

The social upheaval first took place in the north of the main island Kyushu, and then spread to Sinai. In Kanto and on Hokkaido, the Jomon culture was still in the foreground.

And another innovation brought this era to Japan: tools and weapons made of metal, bronze or iron. The latter were exported from Korea via a first international trade. The cultivation of rice also began to involve various irrigation systems for the fields as well as for local housing estates. The Japanese dug ditches for this purpose, which regularly checked the proper functioning of the inhabitants in its vicinity.

The habits of making music changed during the Yayoi period. The elaborately ornate flame patterns of Jomon ceramics were now deviated from. More simplicity and elegance were in demand. This change can be explained by the strong Korean influence on Japan.

Japanese society also changed as a result of the influence China and Korea exerted on Japan. The first social hierarchies emerged.

The basic framework of Yayoi society consisted of a combination of three layers: the Uji in the first place, then the Be who obeyed them, and finally the servants of the Yatsuko who surrendered to them.

The most powerful class of this epoch were the Uji. As the translation of the term suggests (clan, family), this social group consisted of families and clans spun together. These confessed to common ancestors, the "Uji-gami". With their influence on politics, but also their wealth, especially in the sense of rural property, the Uji represented the upper class of Japan. The "Uji no kami", the eldest, took over the leading function within the most highly regarded family. Members of other Uji clans also had to obey him.

Throughout history, some Uji clans have claimed a monopoly of power over other neighbouring families. These hierarchies are seen by historians as an early form of local politics, as they gave rise to various responsibilities.

The Be were supposedly free workers, but obliged to the Uji. Mainly active in agriculture, the "Kakibe" (workers) took care of rice cultivation and fishing. They earned their income for their own use and that of their superiors. But the Be could also act as employees of the state: Interpreters, writers and fortune tellers were the professions that the Be practiced.

The Yatsuko were the social underclass of the still young Japan. They were slaves. As servants of the Uji, they belonged to the unfree. Historically, about five per cent of the population at that time belonged to the Yatsuko. Often, they were used by their masters for servants' errands.

Antiquity (300 - 1192 A.D.)

Kofun-Period (300 – 538)

The large Shinto hill graves ("Kofun") are an impressive testimony of Japanese antiquity. One example is the tomb of Emperor Nintoku-Tenno (313-399).

During the Kofun period, the predominant centre of power was in the province of Yamato, which was located in the present-day prefecture of Nara. It was here that the basic features of the feudal, three-tiered social system spread. Gradually, this development spread to the whole of Japan.

Yamato-Clan

The term Yamato ("great harmony") has a complex, important meaning for Japanese people. In general, it refers to ancient Japan with its specific cultural characteristics. But Yamato is also an expression of the rule of influential ancient families. This went beyond the emperor's sphere of influence.

Yamato society changed during the Kofun period. Enemies between the Uji families could only be settled insufficiently. Buddhism drove a big wedge between the most powerful clans of the epoch, the Soga family, the Mononobe and the Nakatomi.

Soga-Family

Members of the Soga family were considered particularly influential in Japanese antiquity. They were also called the true masterminds of Japan's politics at the time. The Soga family; particularly devoted to Buddhism, fomented conflict with other Japanese clans, especially the conservative Nakatomi family.

As one of the most powerful families of the Uji, they placed their clan eldest (O-omi), who was also empowered to give instructions to the other families. 540 A.D. Soga no Iname was the first Soga to be appointed eldest. His two daughters were made available for marriage to the Emperor Kimmei Tenno (509-575).

The main purpose of Soga at Yamatos Court was to monitor imports and exports, and also to warehouse tribute payments. Thus Soga gained useful insights into the foreign policy relations of Japan, China and Korea. Other responsibilities included decisions on the order of succession, government measures, and foreign policy. Around 522 A.D., Buddhism came up, as religion had the potential to expand the political power of yoga. The supremacy of Shintoism, with its numerous gods, was dammed up because Buddha was classified as a more powerful authority. Buddhism weakened the other families, such as the Mononobe clan, which established its power and rank in military society through the descent of Shinto gods.

The dispute over religion, especially at the political level, lasted for decades and was a troubled time for Yamato. In 587 AD, the Soga defeated the Mononobe. Buddhism was unrivalled in this position as the state religion. For the next 70 years, he thus established the Soga clan as the greatest ruler of Yamato, since these underpinned their leadership through Buddhist theories.

The introduction of Buddhism cripplingly suppressed the Shinto rite of the Kofun tombs. Some nobles and the general people erected the burial mounds until the seventh century. Despite this, the Kofun period was historically replaced by the Asuka period in 538 AD.

Asuka period (538 – 710)

First linguistic influences, like the Chinese script, found their way into the Japanese area with Buddhism. Through the introduction of a tax system and a centralized administration, Japan gained the first features of a state system based on the Chinese model.

Asuka-kyo was the city where Empress Suiko (554 - 628), a niece of the Soga family, resided during this epoch. She was represented by the regent Shotoku-Taishi (574 - 622) in all state affairs.

The power of the government dwindled further and further due to the strong noble families. A mood of upheaval spread in Japan: The people demanded reforms.

If it were for the regent Shotoku-Taishi, the old social order of the three strata would come to an end. In 604 A.D., he proclaimed the first Japanese constitution, consisting of 17 articles, in order to elevate Japan to a monarchy with an official structure.

As a direct descendant of the sun goddess "Amaterasu", he titled himself "Tenno" (son of heaven). This emperor's title had its origin in China, and is still valid today.

In 607, despite his Shinto title, the emperor declared Buddhism the main religion of Japan. He had the first Buddhist temple built a short time later on the island of Honshu.

An important innovation took place at the court: Official posts were no longer to be obtained by inheritance, which weakened the nobility for a short time.

Scholars travelled to the neighbouring country, which Shotoku-Taishi hoped would provide him with further insights into the country's religion and politics. This strengthened the cultural alliance of both countries and helped Japan to a new political orientation.

Shotoku-Taishi died in 622, plunging Japan into renewed unrest. They resulted in the end of the rule of the Soga family. The Nakatomi family gained control of Japan with Nakatomi no Kamatari (614 - 669 AD) and Prince Naka-no-Oe (later Tenji-Tenno) under Emperor Kotoku. The rapprochement of Japanese politics with the Chinese model was continued with them and the Taika reform introduced in 645.

Taika-Reform (645 – 702 / 718)

The Taika reform transformed the state into a centralist organ. Japan became an absolutist monarchy, true to the Chinese model of the Sui and T'ang dynasties. The most important innovations for the citizens were, among other things, the introduction of the Chinese annual count, a new aristocratic hierarchy and the abolition of unfree groups, such as the Yatsu-ko.

The annual count, which was based on foreign exchange, changed with the change of the throne, but also with bad omens.

According to the Taika reform, private land ownership was to be transferred to the government, but this did not prevent the clergy and nobility from further expanding their property and gaining power. It failed because of the nationwide enforcement by the central government.

The purpose of the reforms was to secure the emperor's absolute supremacy. To this end, high-ranking officials were obliged to swear unrestricted loyalty to the ruling emperor. In the sense of a fiefdom, estates could be assigned to the nobility for use by the tenno.

Also, with China as a model, the reform introduced a new tax system. In addition, Japan's capital moved to Naniwa (Osaka).

During the Asuka period, the first collections of laws were created. Two of them, the Taiho Code (701) and the Yoro Code (718), were adopted almost unchanged from China. The integration into Japan was difficult, but these laws applied for the first time in the whole Japanese empire, which should promote the development of a strong central government.

In spite of the desired changes with the help of the Taika reform, or the 17 articles that led away from the aristocratic rule, the state and social structures of the Yamato culture persisted until modern times. Especially, the original families of the Uji class retained their elders as leaders and mediators between rival clans.

Taiho-Kodex (701)

The Taiho Code was named after the annual motto Taiho, which was applied from 701 - 703. The structure of the imperial court was to change as a result. Two sections were created: One section dealt with religious matters; the other section dealt with worldly matters. The Jingi-Kan (divine section) was superior to the Daijo-Kan (secular faction). Interesting is the strong connection of the Jingi-Kan to Shinto-ism. Buddhism and its temples were not administered by him, unlike the Shinto shrines with their associated religious ceremonies.

The so-called city council took care of the secular tasks of the government within the framework of the Daijo-Kan. The head of the council was the chancellor (Daijo-Daijin). The city council consisted of different ministers, who were alternately set up by the altogether eight ministries. Furthermore, the council included four major councils (Dainagon) and three small councils (Shonagon), which corresponded with the chancellor.

In addition, the Taiho Code defined the various offices of the Ministry and their tasks. The division of the Japanese Empire into different provinces was laid down in writing. Each province got a governor, who had to take care of the political and administrative tasks there. A province consisted of several districts, which in turn provided an official who took care of the government affairs there. This included the collection of taxes and the documentation of the local population and its distribution of land. The district population could consist of up to 50 families, each with a head.

By introducing a mint, the new empress Gemmei-tenno (660 - 721), the fourth daughter of Tenji-Tennos, helped Japan to a new currency consisting of copper and silver coins.

In 708, the capital moved again, this time to Heijo-kyo (Nara). Nara was to remain the home of the imperial court for the next 75 years, offering the Japanese people certain political stability.

Nara period (710 – 794)

Nara was crowned the first permanent capital of Japan by the 43rd empress. With a growing interest in poetry, as well as fine craftsmanship around ceramics and silk, a large array of Japanese art and art articles developed at that time, which can still be found in many museums today.

The Chinese models, in this case, the city of Chang´an, were also followed in the construction of the new capital. The surrounding provinces of Naras were connected by a newly built road network. This expanded the area controlled by the emperor, as a better infrastructure was provided by increased mobility, for example for imperial officials.

Nara's population increased horrendously, records document show numbers of about 200,000 citizens.

For the common people, the belief in Shintoism and agriculture were still important pillars of society. But Chinese influences, especially with regard to Japanese writing, could not be dismissed. The Nara period is the era of Japanese literature and poetry. The history of the emperors, including their long line of ancestors, was recorded in writing. Chinese characters of the Kanji script were often used.

Buddhism was anchored in everyday life with the construction of the temples, financed by the state. The different rites, both dominating religions, intermingled especially in rural regions.

The second successor of Gemmei-tennos, her grandson Shomu-tenno (701 - 756), continued to stand up for Buddhism by donating power to the monasteries of Naras. In addition, he established various schools dealing with the spread of Buddhism among the common people. Despite this, there was a gap between the urban and rural population. City dwellers, mostly scholars, could study in China with a special exit permit, and thus had greater access to education. The common people did not get any privileges of this kind.

Konin-tenno (709 - 782), reigned as a descendant of Tenji-Tennos from 770 - 781. He counteracted the power of the emperor, which had been retained by the Taika reform, by ascribing the ownership of the lands back to the nobility. With this, he originally wanted to ensure loyalty within the nobility, but he only lost more of his own sovereignty.

From a military point of view, there were important innovations for the Japanese Empire in 792. New soldiers were recruited from the ranks of the lower nobility to counteract the unrest in the north and east of Japan. These were triggered by the Emishi (or Yezo) people who lived in those regions.

Emishi people

The ethnic group from the northeast of Japan was hostile to the Yamato state. From a scientific point of view, it is not clear whether the Emishi are descendants of the Ainu. The spread of the power relations of Yamatos pushed the Emishi further and further out of their original habitat.

The battles that the Emishi fought mainly for goods, food and their survival lasted until about 800 AD. The Yamato people wanted to exterminate the Emishi, which they almost succeeded in doing. A few survivors capitulated and were able to live on. But their resistance did not end there. Also, long time later, fights still took place with the Japanese of the Yamato Empire.

Slowly but surely, the Yamato people began to infiltrate the Emishi, so that they finally lost their independence and had to integrate themselves into the state structure of Japan.
Towards the end of the Nara period, the capital of the imperial court was moved again after a long time. In 784, the government moved to Nagaoka, only to move to Heian-kyo (Kyoto) ten years later, heralding the beginning of the Heian period.

Heian period (794 – 1192)

The Heian period is regarded as Japan's cultural heyday, as Japanese culture increasingly differentiated itself from China. Politics gradually broke away from Buddhism, but no final separation was to be expected.

The Heian period can be divided into an early and a late period. The late Heian period is also called the Fujiwara period in historical literature.

The Japanese monk Kukai (774 - 835), also known as Kobo-Daishi, is a revered figure in Japanese religious history. With his travels to Shingon in China, dated 806 A.D., he is one of the greatest mediators of Chinese religious culture in Japan. There, he got to know the form of Vajrayana Buddhism anew and brought it to the Japanese Empire.

Mandalas are an important part of the Shingon religion. This also had an effect on the architecture of their places of worship, which had especially symmetrical elements. The Muroji temple from the ninth century comes closest to this architectural style, as the Japanese also sought inspiration in Chinese architecture here.

The cultural emancipation of Japan from China found its origin in the Heian period, as the Japanese language and writing became more and more established, especially in scholarly circles.

Kanbun, an intellectual language written in Kanji, was replaced by Kana, whose characters represented a simplified form of Kanji. Kana is subdivided into the Hiragana and Katakana forms, which are still known today. Nowadays, Hiragana is used alongside Kanji as one of the everyday scripts in Japan, while Katakana is often used for foreign and loan words. At that time, Hiragana was the writing of the noble women and Katakana the writing of the men. Since both scripts consist of syllable characters, the spoken language could be well documented with them. This changed Japanese literature by creating new genres.

The Waka were Japanese poems, which were written in the colloquial language of the time with characters of the Hiragana. They enjoyed great popularity as an alternative to poems in the Chinese language, and mostly dealt with the subject of love.

There are two kinds of Waka: Tanka and Haiku.

The Tanka contains five lines with a fixed number of syllables. A haiku consists of three lines, and is a very aesthetic poem form. Besides love, it deals with nature and the emotional world of the author.

Such waka opened up new possibilities, especially for the women of Japanese society, as they were able to express themselves publicly with this type of poetry. Ladies of the court, as well as several "concubines" of the Japanese emperor, received a voice in this way.

These developments were not least promoted by male court citizens, e.g. Emperor Uda (867 - 931) was very open to the poetry of women at his court.

Also, the typical Japanese picture roles had their origin in the Heian period, the so-called Emaki. Strongly influenced by Buddhist scrolls, they even created new offices, the Jishaedokoro (Office of Temple Art) and Kyuteiedokoro (Imperial Office of Painting). As members of these offices, commissioned artists earned their living by making emaki for the court nobility. But laymen also had the opportunity to train as Emaki painters at the imperial court.

The Late Heian Period

The Fujiwara family had a far-reaching influence on Japanese politics in the Heian period because, they were direct descendants of the powerful Nakatomi family. Emperor Tenji (626 - 672) gave the clan his new name while he was dying.

Their influence began with the elevation of Nakatomi no Kamatari (614 - 669) to the government of the Asuka period. Their rivals included the Tachibana clan. The Fujiwara infiltrated the imperial court by forming useful family ties.

In the late Heian period, the Minamoto clan and the Taira clan dominated the Japanese aristocracy.

The Minamoto clan consisted primarily of sons of the imperial family who were not eligible for succession to the throne. They were given the same surname for bureaucratic simplification. The same applied to members of the Taira clan. The conflict arose when Emperor Toba (1103 - 1156) and Emperor Sutoku (1119 - 1164) resided at the court with Emperor Konoe (1139 - 1155) at the same time. After Konoe's assassination, it was unclear who would ascend the throne. The Minamoto clan supported Sutoku, while the Taira supported Toba's opinion that Go-Shirakawa (1127 - 1192) should become the new Japanese emperor. The family realms were intricately interwoven because Emperor Toba was the father of Sutoku and Go-Shirakawa. When Toba died, two camps formed and a civil war broke out. The battles were fought by samurai chosen by the families themselves.

The Minamoto suffered great losses after the Battle of Hogen, which took place in Kyoto in 1156. The Taira were able to secure their place at the emperor's court, and continue the policy of the Fujiwara Clan. But survivors of the Minamoto family were not yet willing to accept defeat. Some fights and a second civil war in 1159 were the consequences of an act of revenge. Although the Minamoto were successful, the Taira managed to maintain their powerful position in the Japanese government. It was only on the threshold of the Middle Ages, in 1185, that the Minamoto won the battle of Danoura, and were able to secure part of the power.

The Middle Ages (1192 – 1603)

With the appointment of Minamoto, no Yorito-mo (1147 - 1199) as the first Shogun in 1192, Japan heralded the Middle Ages. This epoch was marked by many battles around power, religion and territorial claim. The emperor subjected himself to the warrior nobility, and had only a formal say in government matters. Depending on the shogun's residence city, the Japanese Middle Ages are divided into the Kamakura period, the Muromachi period and the Azuchi-Momomaya period.

Shoguns (1192 – 1868)

The term Shogun can be translated as "military commander". This new social grouping displaced the court nobility from its supremacy, and called the members of the warrior nobility onto the scene.

The emperor was unofficially submissive to the shoguns from 1192 to 1868. The Shogun, the head of the warrior nobility, ruled almost unrestrictedly over Japan throughout the Middle Ages, and into the early modern period. Rivalries with the degraded court nobility and the followers of the emperor were the order of the day.

Until the beginning of the 17th century, this complicated power structure meant an uncertain time for the Japanese population. The Shoguns fought among themselves to maintain their positions of power, and became entangled in escalating battles.

The Samurai

The samurai belonged to the Japanese knighthood, and were subject to the shogun. They also belonged to the warrior aristocracy (Buke), which stood opposite the court aristocracy (Kuge).

Originally, the Japanese army was formed from peasant recruits. But then, more and more men from the land nobility of lower class registered for military service. Dangerous, brutal fighters with their own code of honour emerged. Also, revolts against their own masters are historically documented.

The reason for the rise in power of the Samurai lies in the way they dealt with property at that time. Originally, the court nobility gave the Samurai properties and lands, so that they could be protected and administered by them. Regionally, the fiefdom of the Samurai became more and more important because they were the local contact for all imperial concerns. As a result, various monopolies of power were formed around individual provinces.

The office of the emperor has lost importance and power again by the shoguns. His throne was still occupied, but it was clear that the true responsibility for Japan's politics lay unofficially with the war commander and his samurai.

In the Middle Ages, the meeting of the Japanese with Europeans who explored the oceans became more frequent. In the period around 1500 – 1550, the first Europeans also travelled to the Japanese islands. Sea farers from Portugal and missionaries brought Christianity to

Japan. Some influential people converted, among them, DaimyooOda Nobunaga, one of the most important shoguns. The Shogunate then adopted a hostile attitude towards Buddhism and destroyed many of its temples.

Kamakura period (1192 bis 1333)

The port city of Kamakura, located south of Tokyo, was the seat of government of the Shogun until the early 12th century.

The imperial court, which continued to be located in Heian-kyo, suffered a lasting loss of power. Through a clever marriage policy, however, the Fujiwara family found the means to continue to participate in important political issues. The rest of the court was allowed to retain its representative, religious and cultural function. The Emperor's task was to formally confirm the political innovations of the Shogunate.

The first Mongol attack on Japan took place in 1274. China and Korea had already won them over. A second invasion was launched in 1281.

The danger could both times be successfully averted by the Japanese army.

Nevertheless, the current Shogunate was so weakened by the attacks that rivals from their own country sensed their chance. In 1336, the Ashikaga family was the new head, and Kyoto was again the capital of Japan.

The scattered systems of rule helped Buddhism find new ways to spread throughout Japan. Various teachings streamed into the country, and the "new Buddhism" was born.

Honen (1133-1212) was one of the most controversial personalities in Japanese religious history because, his followers showed little tolerance for other Buddhist branches. He spread the new theories together with Shinran (1173 - 1262). He further developed Honens teachings and founded the Jodo Shinshu School. Until today, his school offers the basis of Buddhist teachings in Japan.

Buddhism opened itself to the broad masses. Simple and understandable teachings developed, including amidism as the most important form of interpretation.

Amidism

This Buddhist reform had its origin already in the Heian period, in the so-called Tendai Buddhism. Amidismis based on the belief in Amida, and its pure land. Also, within this branch of religion, there were variations. Thus, within Amidism, different groups developed, whose core consisted of the same religious writings.

Amidism interpreted the everyday life of the Japanese population on an understandable religious level, and thus, also helped the simple living people to more spirituality. This also explained the popularity of this religion. It was deliberately preached in public places in order to reach all classes.

A radical form of amidism also emerged. It was tried to prevent this by making every believer confess to the versatility of the Buddhist schools. If one did not do this, one could not expect any tolerance from the others. Followers of this faith were stamped as fundamentalists and partly executed.

Honen and Shinran looked at the radical orientation of Amidism with criticism since one should respect all religious directions as a true Amida believer. They had to bear the consequences of this development by going into exile for several years.

Peasants and members of the lower land nobility instrumentalized religion to draw attention to the grievances of their way of life. They organized uprisings and demanded reforms regarding the rigid social structure and the court nobility.

The shoguns and the affluent urban population believed in Zen Buddhism, and had few points of contact with amidism.

Muromachi period (1338 – 1573)

The subsequent Muromachi period turned out to be a particularly unstable, troubled era for Japan: There was a civil war between North and South as a result of the unequal distribution of power between the samurai, the emperor and the rich elite of the country.

With the arrival of the Europeans, the first firearms arrived in Japan. In the end, they pushed the samurai out of active service. The Ashikaga clan took over the Shogunate during this period.

After the samurai could no longer participate in battles, they turned to the arts. Especially, the theatre was promoted by samurai. The change of the Samurai to an intellectually inspired social group promoted the education of different traditions, which are firmly anchored in the Japanese culture until today. Tea ceremonies were upgraded as an important ritual in their social importance. As a form of meditation, they were intended to free the human mind from all the unrest of everyday life.
Buddhist monastery followers were also given

the opportunity to go on trade trips to China. China exported its goods to Japan, including ceramics, books and silk fabrics. The Chinese knowledge about crafts, economy and politics was brought to the Japanese court by the travellers and made use of.

The Japanese social structure changed. Within the country, a well-situated middle class developed, which was mainly at home in the city. A leasing system, consisting of the Sakunin (tenant) and the subtenant (Gesakunin), developed. This new hierarchy displeased the lower classes. Combined with the reckless conduct of loss-making power struggles within the nobility, it was above all the peasants who struggled with great poverty.

The Sengoku period (1467 – 1573)

1467 heralded the "time of the quarrelling empires" (Sengoku-jidai), which would last for about 100 years. The Ashikaga clan lost a lot of power at the beginning of this period. 1467 to 1477, a civil war took place in Japan, the Onin war. The quarrels escalated between different clans who had their lands administered. Kyoto was badly affected by the fighting. Japan broke up into many different provinces ruled by independent princes (Sengoku-Daimyo). The governors previously appointed by the central government were no longer relevant. Numerous disputes between the princes, whose expanded power is due to their land ownership, shattered Japan into a diffuse web of different territorial claims.

Azuchi-Momomaya period (1573 – 1603)

The reunification of Japan took place during the Azuchi-Momoyama period. Important personalities of this epoch are Oda Nobunaga, Tokugawa Ieyasu and Toyotomi Hideyoshi, the successor of Nobunaga. They forced the unitary state with military means.

The name Azuchi comes from the military fortress Nobunagas. Hideyoshi also lived in the city of Momoyama.

Nobunaga's fortress adapted to the military changes that brought European firearms to Japan. The prince, who took Kyoto in 1568, strengthened his influence by exchanging the shogun of the Ashikaga clan for Yoshiaki, a friend of the military radel. He was also able to assert himself successfully against other princes in the region, and thus, successfully end the Sengoku period.

Nobunaga was at war with Buddhist monasteries. When he began to destroy temples, the other monasteries, although the other monasteries had their own military forces, were forced to submit to him. This greatly weakened the power of the monasteries throughout the country.

In 1573, Nobunaga deprived the Shogunate of his power to put an end to the Shogunate for the time being.

The Azuchi-Momoyama period was marked by violence and war. Nobunaga's dictatorial control brought with it many battles and deaths.

In 1582, he died under unclear circumstances. Hideyoshi, coming from poorer circumstances, became Nobunaga's successor. He made it his life's work to continue Nobunaga's plan of a united Japan. He inherited an impressive military power - the army of over 230,000 soldiers intimidated many hostile princes. With the last battle in 1590, Hideyoshi had successfully completed the unification of Japan. After this success, Hideyoshi was ready to give back land to the princes, and thus, a certain amount of power in the sense of an inner political stabilization. New taxes were introduced and the estates were divided among themselves.

This, however, did not lead to a final settlement of the disputes, as the lower classes, in particular, were in the grip of resistance. Hideyoshi's intervention pushed the peasants back into their villages.

The samurai and their shoguns, who had been left relatively powerless until then, were now tasked with securing peace within Japan and stopping the uprisings.

Hideyoshi's megalomania was particularly evident in his attempts to conquer neighbouring countries, such as Korea and China by means of military troops. Thus, he stirred up unrest in the border areas until his death in 1598.

His successor was Tokugawa Ieyasu, a military commander from his own ranks. Thus, the warrior nobility regained its supremacy, and a new Shogun established himself as head of government. The period of Tokugawa rule was particularly long for Japanese history: for almost 200 years they ruled the country on the highest front. Tokugawa Ieyasu's political style can be described as moderate, in contrast to his predecessors. Japan began to stabilize both within the country and in the border region.

Momoyama became a city of trade and culture. Portugal proved to be a loyal trading partner. But the Portuguese also pursued their own religious agenda.

The seafarers who resided in Japan began to missionize small parts of the peasant population. Around 1582, Christianity thus had about 150,000 members in Japanese society. Since a small part converted to fundamentalist Catholicism, the Japanese attitude to European visitors changed rapidly. Persecutions up to executions were the result.

Early modern age

Edo period (also: Tokugawa period, 1603 – 1868)

Tokugawa Ieyasu moved the Japanese capital again, this time to Edo (today: Tokyo). He heralded the Edo period, the early modern period of Japanese history. After times of unrest and civil wars, a very long period of peace finally followed. This was also the period of Japan's isolation.

For 200 years, Japan kept itself under lock and key with the world (Sakoku). Only the Chinese got the exception to stay in the country. Japanese who lived abroad had to stay there. In their home country, they would otherwise face the death penalty. The citizens were also not allowed to leave the country.

For the Christians in Japan, the dangers became more acute. In the meantime, the Western religion had 500,000 members. The fear of persecution and execution was part of the daily life of a Japanese Christian. It was justified: Around 1603, the executions led to the almost complete extinction of religion on Japanese territory.

The Edo period was the epoch of urban development. Many cities, especially Edo, expanded and developed a stable infrastructure. The road network was extended, and schools and temples were built. The population of Tokyo increased rapidly. In comparison to other big cities, Tokyo probably had one million inhabitants by 1721. The city's favourable location was certainly one of the reasons for its rapid growth. The bay of Edo was well protected, and the city was far enough away from the dangerous interior of Japan. For example, raids by the Mongolian people were almost impossible.

The trade routes of Japan all met in the Edos area, which was also a reason for the relocation of the capital. As so often, the nobility and the city population profited most from these innovations. The vassals became richer and richer, the poor in the countryside poorer and poorer.

Economic structures changed and encouraged unrest in the part of the population. The taxes were very high, and so there were isolated revolts of the peasants. A new corporative society emerged.

The four-stand system

The upper class was made up of samurai, who were meanwhile connoisseurs of the fine arts, and rarely active in military service. They were divided into the sword and warrior nobility and enjoyed great prestige.

Interestingly, the peasants (Hyokusho) belonged to the middle class because they produced their own goods. Here, a big difference shows up to the western way of thinking: Rice farmers received a lot of honour because they ensured one of the most important pillars of Japanese society, the staple food rice. The importance of certain works, which had to be carried out for the benefit of all, was therefore taken into account in the hierarchy of occupations. Craftsmen (Shokunin) such as potters and weavers belonged to the lower middle class. Merchants (Akino) were members of the lower class, since they only sold the goods, and did not produce them themselves. Merchants enjoyed growing prosperity due to the lively trade in the cities, despite their inferior position. The merchants of the city were also called Chonin.

As the Chonin wanted to expand their trade internationally, a desire for reform arose in 1850 to put an end to Japan's isolation from the outside world. However, this was a thorn in the side of the ruling shoguns, and so, the desired opening of the borders did not take place for the time being. Through the entry of mainly Chinese and Dutch traders, who had no interest in a missionary work of the Japanese population and were thus permitted in the country, the Chonin were able to establish trade relations and increase their wealth despite their remoteness from the rest of the world.

Art and Culture in the Edo Period

The clear division of tasks and social structure, combined with international isolation, have allowed Japan's art and culture to develop comprehensively. The citizens of the city were very fond of the arts, especially Japanese theatre (Kabuki).

The theatre of Japan captivates by its elaborate realization, the striking costumes, as well as the musical and dancing influences. The figures of Kabuki are loud, expressive and are performed only by male actors. The main theme is the history of Japan. This is impressively brought to the stage. To this day, Kabuki is considered a Japanese cultural asset, and was declared a UNESCO World Heritage Site in 2005.

Sumo

In the field of sport, Sumo spread throughout the country during the Edo period and became Japan's national sport. The first wrestling fights took place during the Nara period within the framework of religious practices. It was not until the Kamakura period that Sumo gained recognition as a martial art. The set of rules differentiated itself and caused a split to the

JuJitsu, a sport which was practiced mainly by the Samurai.

Japanese poetry and literature flourished during the time of peace. It was brought to the people with the help of newly introduced magazines, the contents of which were poems and woodcut illustrations. This took place under the strict eyes of the shoguns, who critically watched the distribution of entertainment magazines. In the context of a new literary movement, the Utagawa School, a union of many Japanese artists, was founded at the end of the Edo period.

It had about 400 members in its heyday, and influenced various techniques of Japanese woodblock printing. Her works include advertising posters for the Kabuki Theater and numerous book illustrations.

The modern age

Meji period (1868 – 1912)

From 1853 to 1854, Japan opened up to the outside world. One reason for this was the arrival of an American fleet on the country's coast under Commander Perry. In 1854, the Kanagawa Treaty was signed, which ensured the supply of American ships to two Japanese ports. In addition, America was allowed to open a consulate, which paved the way for other European states to Japan. Attempts by the shoguns to mess with the foreign rulers failed because of their technical inferiority. After the opening, Japan quickly managed to take a self-confident position in the world structure, unlike e.g. India, which fell victim to the colonial powers.

The time of the Shoguns came to an end with the Meji Restoration. Tokugawa Yoshinobu (1837 - 1913) left his office as the last Shogun of Japan in 1868. The only fifteen-year-old emperor Meji (1852 - 1912) regained the power of his throne. Japan wanted to appear sovereign before the European powers and with a united government. The Shoguns, with their traditional way of thinking, stood in the way of correspondence with Europe and had to give way. Unlike in Europe, this took place without violent uprisings and revolutions. For the Japanese, the restoration of the imperial office felt more like a return to the old order, and is therefore also called restoration.

But the opening of the borders did not have only positive effects on Japan. It quickly became clear that Japan's armed forces could not keep up with international competition. Researchers should now travel to Europe to see the state structure and way of life there. They then presented the useful evaluations of these excursions to the emperor.

The four-tier system came to an end, the tax system reformed. The feudal princes were expropriated, and had to repay their land to the emperor. They were allowed to retain their positions as administrators.

School attendance and compulsory military service were introduced. The latter meant that the status of the warrior nobility, and thus, the samurai finally lost their power.

Meji reforms

The political model was Prussia, so that their entire collection of laws was taken over by the Japanese. The tendency towards discipline and uniformity, and the strong military underpinnings of society, appealed to the Japanese members of the government.

But the people did not agree with these developments, so that around 1870, protests formed increasingly. The interest in politics now seemed to be reflected in the population as a whole, and the rebellion for co-determination increased. The first popular parties against the nobility emerged. These organized themselves into a counter-party.

The resistance of the population led to a reorganization of the state apparatus. The government created a parliament with two chambers according to the British model. Despite this, the emperor retained unrestricted power. The parliament served rather representative purposes, and as a means to calm the Japanese citizens. Nevertheless, Japan is an astonishing example of a rapid restructuring of power relations with democratic features, and thus, historically possesses a unique selling point.

Meji Constitution

On 11.2.1889, after eight years of preparation, the new constitution came into force. Japan became a constitutional monarchy.

The transfer of government and imperial offices was to continue on a hereditary basis. The constitution could only be changed with the approval of the Reichstag. The structural structure of the Reichstag, with its various houses, was described in detail. The protection and veneration of the emperor are also an important part of the constitution.

Every Japanese citizen was free from that time on to profess his religion and own property. The tax system and the judiciary also found new regulations.

In 1947, the Meji Constitution was the basis for the reformation of Japan after the Second World War.

Modernization of the military

Arms exports helped the Japanese army to modernize rapidly during the Meji period. The rapid adoption of modern technology enabled Japan to quickly establish itself as a serious opponent of Europe. The samurai had no part in this modernization, as they dismissed firearms as dishonourable, and thus, had no chance against technically advanced armies. By such a weakening of the Samurai, the emperor did not have to fear any internal political competition regarding his monopoly of power.

With its growing military power, Japan began to acquire new territories. In 1870, Japan occupied archipelagos near Taiwan and climbed the Kuril mountain range in the Russian border region.

When Japan met China around 1890, during the Tong-hak uprising in Korea, the Chinese-Japanese war began. This lasted from 1894 to 1895. Japan managed to acquire more land, including Shantung and Seoul. Taiwan could also be annexed.

Russia crystallized as the next great opponent. From 1904 to 1905, the Russian-Japanese war took place, from which Japan emerged again with newly won territories. For the first time, an Asian great power defeated a European one, which was very impressive for the international state society and earned Japan respect.

With these two successes, the island state asserted itself in international society and became a powerful imperial power.

The Meji period is the time of Japan's industrialization. Japan is often cited as the only non-European example where an industrial revolution was possible in such a short time.

It is often historically unclear what exactly caused the industrial innovations in Japan, as agriculture and new technologies underwent almost simultaneous change. Thus, Meji restoration is not seen by scientists as a consequence of industrialization, but as a cause.

As far as the economy was concerned, Japan did not seem to be able to get away from its influential families: power monopolies were once again formed, this time, around the clans of Mitsui, Yasuda and Sumitomo. The Mitsui Group, which was founded in 1947, had its origins in this period and still represents a powerful group of companies in Japan today. The Yasuda family founded the Yasuda Mutual Life Insurance Company and Fuji Bank in 1880, among others. Yoko Ono is one of the most internationally famous representatives of this family clan. Sumitomo Masatomo (1585 - 1652) founded the Sumitomo Group in 1615, an influential group of companies in the mining, iron and steel industries that still exists today. Free competition was not possible in those days due to these supremacies. These entrepreneurial groups still bear the expression Zaibatsu today. The money for industrialization was collected by taxes. Some of the sums also flowed into the coffers of the aforementioned corporate groups.

Japan imported many engineers and scientists from Europe in order to further advance progress. They acquired their knowledge and made prototypes of their own machines, which were an improved version of those from Europe.

These economic innovations were largely financed by the state, but also by private investors. The system is exemplary for the Meji period, and still runs through Japan's economic structures today.

Taisho period (1912 - 1926)

The emperor of the Taisho period, Yoshihito (1879 - 1926), was physically and mentally handicapped due to early childhood meningitis. In history, he is often portrayed as a weak emperor, who only filled the transitional period between Emperor Meji and Hirohito.

Such a reserved emperor had the advantage that Japan could allow itself new cultural freedoms. The West found its way more and more into Japan. Statesmen who had previously dressed in traditional garb now wore Western military uniforms.

The Taisho period was the time of Japanese imperialism. The Versailles Peace Congress transferred the former German concessions located in China to Japan.

Takashi Hara (1856 - 1921) was the first head of state of bourgeois origin. His term of office included the first cabinet formed by parties. He was the only democratically elected prime minister and Christian leader until 1954, which earned him many enemies on the conservative side. In 1921, he was murdered by a nationalist assassin at Tokyo station.

Rice riots (July-September 1918)

The rice riots were caused by a large discrepancy in the price of rice, which the farmers received compared to the final price. The First World War and the inflation associated with it caused many state estates to raise their prices, and rice as a staple food had the most far-reaching effects on society.

The result was increased poverty and simultaneous famine among the farmers. Protests increased exorbitantly. Takashi Hara benefited retroactively from the instability that prevailed in Japan during the rice riots. His seizure of power was made possible because there was no alternative to the office of the ruler, and the old government had to resign.

Fascination of the West

When it was recognized that the Netherlands played a lesser role at the international level than expected due to its size, larger European countries such as Germany or Great Britain were turned to. Germany triggered a great fascination; the language and the German spirit had a high position in Japanese society. Philosophers like Immanuel Kant found their way into Japanese bookstores. Sympathy for German culture continued until the Second World War.

Europe had a lasting influence not only on literature, but also on painting. The Japanese painter Kobayashi Kiyichika (1847 - 1915) oriented himself towards Western painting without disregarding Japanese traditions such as woodcuts.

The Japanese scholars discovered humanism and spread it throughout the country. A leftist group developed, which among other things, pleaded for the right to vote for men. This movement joined together to form the Socialist Party of Japan, which lasted only one year. Despite this, a small group of radical left-wing scholars was able to hold their own and found support, especially among Chinese students in Tokyo. From there, the first plans for the Chinese revolution started.

Japan in the First World War (1914 - 1918)

For a long time, Germany proved to be an ideal source of inspiration for Japan when it came to politics. However, the good relationship between the two great powers came to an abrupt end in 1895. The German government had a great interest in areas in Asia. The Liaotung Peninsula, which Japan successfully claimed for itself after the Chinese-Japanese War, was to be denied to the Empire again, as Germany feared that Japan could grow dangerously.

When two German missionaries became victims of murder, Germany had enough excuses to threaten Japan militarily. The then Emperor Wilhelm II occupied the Kiatschou Bay, a part of the Chinese east coast, from 1.11.1897. Thus Germany had taken the first, tactically cleverly situated Asian territory. Soon, the German Empire expanded to the Chinese territory around the base, and built the port of Tsingtao, where the navy could moor and dock during the war.

This development also displeased other great powers in Europe, especially England. They saw Japan as an ally against the Germans, and so, the Anglo-Japanese alliance was founded on 30.01.1902. Great Britain thus helped Japan to a more powerful position in world politics.

Japan's military strength increased. The then minister Okuma Shigenobu cultivated the relationship with England because he hoped for further advantages for the empire. Among other things, this was intended to stabilize domestic politics and avoid uprisings.

However, the alliance with the British also brought with it its obligations. When England participated in the First World War from 4.8.1914, Japan should offer support. Japan regarded this as a possibility to weaken Germany in its position as colonial ruler. The ultimatum given to Germany on 15.8.1914 to withdraw all its ships from the waters of China and Japan should help.

The Germans were visibly shocked by this. The Japanese people had once worshipped them and regarded them as role models. Japan's reputation began to deteriorate rapidly in the German Empire, and the Japanese were portrayed as hypocrites and traitors. The Prussian-Japanese trade treaty, called in 1861, was dissolved. A few days later, on 23 August 1914, Japan finally declared war on Germany and began to besiege the German port of Tsingtao with the help of the British. This turned out to be a successful move, as Germany surrendered at the beginning of November, and the country was again released to the Japanese. The German citizens who lived in Tsingtao were allowed to stay there and do their work.

Japan also participated in the occupation of German colonies in the Pacific, which spread to the various islands of the ocean. Despite the pressure of the English, but also the French, the Japanese government did not send troops directly to Europe.

After the successful expulsion of the German forces from the surrounding regions, Japan turned to its Asian competitors. Half a year after the start of World War II, China received 21 demands from the Japanese government in which Japan claimed economic and political supremacy. Since China did not have much power at that time, the then government was inclined to submit to the demands, and thus, to be pushed into the position of a semi-colonial dependence on Japan. In 1916, Japan operated in Asia without restrictions after Chinese consent. Trade with Inner Mongolia and other partners originally left to the Chinese flourished.

Japan's position as a useful partner of Germany in Asia was not forgotten, and so the Germans did everything they could to cement relations. However, a possible peace between the once friendly countries was thwarted by England.

At the end of the First World War in 1918, when the Treaty of Versailles was called up, Japan was given the occupied Pacific islands, such as the Marshall and Caroline Islands. Furthermore, Japan should not exceed a certain fleet size. Guam had claimed the USA for itself and had expanded as a military base. After Chinese-Japanese negotiations, Kiatschou returned to China's possession. Japan then cancelled the 21 demands, and gave China more sovereignty again.

Japan's influence in China continued. Since the then Soviet Union also saw potential for its own interests here, Japan was classified as economically special.

Japan's breakaway from the local climes and simultaneous immersion in colonial politics strengthened the country enormously. The occupied territories, especially the German Tsingtao, proved to be very large and tactically valuable. Germany claimed the entire province of Shandong for itself - this power now fell to Japan.

The world was divided among the colonial powers: In the south the British, in the north the Japanese.

It is notable that the losses to the Japanese Empire during the First World War were small, if one compares the influence and profit gained by the country through intelligent troop policies. This was also made clear to the great powers of Europe at that time. Japan thus gained far-reaching respect and a firm foothold in the world politics of the time.

Showa period (1926 - 1989)

The Showa period is the time of Emperor Hirohito (1901 - 1989), the son of the previously deceased Tenno of the Taisho period. Showa translated means "Enlightened Peace", a term that the Japanese awarded to the emperor of that time as a form of recognition. Hirohito's reign proved to be very long and extended far beyond the Second World War. A Colonial policy was pursued on a large scale until 1929, when the world economic crisis also left its mark in Japan.

The rule of the colonial rulers led to an expansion of the Japanese territory desired by the people. China had to pay for this once again, and the Manchuria crisis arose. Here, as so often, the Japanese military unfolded its power over the emperor, who was rather critical of the war. Despite this, his term of office proved to be extremely violent and militaristic.

In 1933, Japan withdrew from the League of Nations, and was able to devote itself entirely to its territorial interests. Shortly before the Second World War, in 1937, a second war broke out between China and Japan. Japan again emerged victoriously and opened up new territories, especially in the southeast of Asia. Reconciliation with Germany had taken place and the three-country alliance, in which Italy still participated, sealed German-Japanese relations around 1940. Now, Japan could no longer avoid sending its troops into European territory.

Japan's role in the Second World War (1939 - 1945)

The desire for a good relationship between the two countries originated in Japan in the 1930s. The fronts with the USSR had hardened, and Japan was looking for a strong partner to possibly take military action against the Soviet regime. Japan pursued territorial interests not only in southeastern Asia, but also in the Russian border region and beyond, trying to establish itself as an island state.

On 25.11.1936, the *Antikominternpakt* was brought into being. This was directed against communism, and thus, subliminally against the

Soviet Union. The contracting parties banned any trade with the USSR under public lock and key, and established a neutral stance in the event of an attack by the Soviet Union.

Other countries joined Germany and Japan, but they were not informed of the additional clauses upon accession. These countries included Hungary, Spain, Bulgaria, Croatia, Finland, Romania and Slovakia.

On the part of the Nazi regime, the alliance with Japan did not have far-reaching significance. Hitler wrote the German-Soviet Non-Aggression Treaty on 22 August 1939, which contained very contrary information to the pact concluded with Japan. The Three-Country Pact and the attack by Nazi Germany on the USSR, however, strengthened Japan's role as a military partner.

Pearl Harbour

Japan's active entry into the Second World War is heralded with the attack on Pearl Harbour on 07.12.1941. Thus, the battles spread over the Pacific. The declaration of war to the USA took place one day later, as contract partner Germany followed in short time and declared the war to the United States likewise.

Despite their alliance, Japan and the NS regime never fought on the same battlefields. Japan's battlefield extended to Asia and the Pacific, while the Nazi regime fought in Europe and North Africa.

When the USA exorbitantly increased its financial resources for the war around 1943, Japan had no chance to maintain its position in the Pacific Ocean. In parallel, the Americans launched their attack on Normandy on 6 June 1944, which weakened Germany enormously, and heralded its surrender.

Japan and the USSR finally concluded an armistice in 1939 until 1945, due to the heavy losses in Manchuria. During this time, Germany attacked Poland.

The number of troops decreased around 1941, so that the Red Army was no longer designed to defend areas close to Japan. Instead, Stalin used all Russian troops to defend the capital

Moscow.

Germany capitulated on 8.5.1945, so that the fighting shifted back to the Pacific. Japan did not follow the NS regime into capitulation, but tried to further defend its imperialist interests.

The dropping of the atomic bomb on Hiroshima and Nagasaki on 6 and 9 August 1945, was one of the biggest cuts in Japan's history. 200,000 people died and the far-reaching consequences of the radiation can still be felt today. The catastrophe brought Japan to surrender on 2.9.1945.

Hiroshima and Nagasaki

Before the First World War, Hiroshima was considered the economic, cultural and military centre of Japan. In the wars between Japan and China, as well as with Russia, the city played an important role as a weapons manufacturer and supplier. It established several militaristic schools and attained prosperity. This position lasted until the Second World War, and made Hiroshima a tactically attractive target for Japan's opponents.

With the tragic event of the atomic bombing, Hiroshima became the first city in history to face such a catastrophe. Since Japan under Hirohito did not bow to the Allies, the then US President of Japan wanted to force Japan's government to surrender. Harry Truman finally promised to claim nuclear weapons for this political goal. It quickly became clear that Hiroshima would be the target of the attack. The 6.8.1945, a Monday, was chosen as day X. "Little Boy", the atomic bomb, exploded in the morning in the center of the city near a hospital.

The extent of the detonation was horrendous. Never before had nuclear weapons been used, and the shock to the Japanese, as well as to the rest of the world, was very deep. The protracted damage caused by radioactive radiation continued for decades to come. For a long time, the area was considered uninhabitable and about 70 percent of all buildings were completely destroyed. What remained was a dead desert landscape, which received the Japanese term Yakenohara.

Despite the tragic events, the Americans were willing to use the atomic bomb a second time, as Japan still did not surrender. This time on 9.8.1945, with the target Nagasaki.

Japan then officially surrendered on 2.9.1945. Before that, Emperor Hirohito announced the news to the Japanese people by means of a radio message. This marked the first personal correspondence of a Japanese emperor with his people. With this, the Second World War was officially ended.

This was followed by the first occupation of Japan by another world power, the USA. The hard-fought islands claimed the Allies for their military presence in the Pacific.

On 3.11.1947, the new constitution under emperor Hirohito was blessed, which exists until today. Although the victorious powers exerted their influence on the government structure of Japan, the constitution has retained some things from the Meji Restoration.

In the new constitution, the Japanese people have full sovereignty. This paved the way for democracy in Japan. Human rights, too, are now enshrined in writing.

Despite all the tragic events around the Second World War, which severely weakened Japan on the one hand, the country managed to develop into the second largest world economic power after 1952, by regaining its sovereignty on the other. The American occupation of the Pacific islands also came to an end.

Japan joined the United Nations in 1956. In addition, at the end of the seventies, the relationship with the People's Republic of China was drastically improved by means of a peace treaty. In 1989, Hirohito ended his term of office with his death. Even today, the emperor enjoys a high reputation among the Japanese people.

Heisei period (1989 - today)

Japan is currently in the Heisei period, the time of peace. Emperor Akihito (1933*), Hirohito's son, made peace his government motto.

On Akihito's agenda are primarily great efforts to reconcile with China, and to build a good political relationship. He was the first emperor to visit the People's Republic in person.

However, Akihito does not show enough remorse for many affected states about his father's war tactics, to which many people in the Asian region fell victim. Only visits to Hiroshima, Nagasaki, as well as Okinawa are regularly attended by the emperor. All these are places where the victims mostly belonged to the Japanese people.

The emperor's office gave up his divinity without comment after the Second World War. The aim was to develop into a democratically influenced form of government. The old traditions should not stand in the way of this. Akihito is the first, purely bourgeois emperor of Japan.

He tries to express this with an unprecedented closeness to the people.

The imperial office has a purely representative function in Japan today.

The head of government is the Prime Minister, currently Shinzo Abe (21.9.1954*). The Liberal Democrats and the so-called Komei Party are involved in the government. The form of government is democratic; all Japanese citizens are entitled to vote after reaching the age of majority.

Japanese democracy

The Japanese Parliament (Kokkai) is the most powerful authority of the government, and consists of two houses: Shugiin, the lower house with 475 members, and Sangiin, the upper house, but with fewer members (242). The lower house is politically superior to the upper house.

In most legal matters, both chambers must give their consent. They also elect the Prime

Minister.

In addition to Parliament, there is the Japanese Cabinet, whose members are elected by the Prime Minister. The members of the Cabinet provide the ministers needed for the various offices and are ordinary citizens. Each of Japan's 47 prefectures is governed by a governor, who mainly deals with regional issues.

Japan had to struggle with many economic setbacks, which slowly but surely separated it from its economic supremacy. In the meantime, China has established itself as a powerful emerging country in world politics and has outstripped the Japanese state. The bubble economy came to an abrupt end during the Heisei era.

Bubble Economy

In the 1980s, a number of speculative transactions took place in Japan, mainly in the real estate and corporate sectors. So-called "bubbles" formed within the Japanese economy. However, these bubbles burst due to disproportionate investments and financing. The

Asian stock market crash in 1990 is attributable to this bubble economy in Japan. The year 1990 thus marked the Japanese crisis.

The crisis, from which Japan has not yet recovered 100 percent, was preceded by a significant economic upturn in the years following the Second World War. Japan entered the world economy and its currency, the yen, gained enormous value in the mid-1970s to late 1980s.

Japan was, because of its innovation and flexibility, a very important trading partner for other world economic powers. Among the leading industries were the electrical and high-tech sectors, due to new technologies. The automotive industry also experienced an upswing in export trade. Thanks to new knowledge in manufacturing, Japan was able to quickly produce many goods, and thus, achieved high export figures. Interest rates, which continued to fall in Japan at that time, were not entirely innocent of this. It was therefore very easy to obtain large loans from the Bank of Japan at low conditions. The prices for company shares and real estate continued to rise in the country. Investments by Japanese companies were the result. In particular, companies that no longer belonged to Japan's most influential tried to take up a new position in the economic structure.

The late 1980s marked the height of Japan's economic recovery, which no investor thought should come to an abrupt end. The value of land and real estate has risen so much that it has even exceeded the value of real estate in the US.

The parallel rise in unemployment, triggered by companies' austerity policies, slowly but surely heralded the Japanese crisis. Condominiums were unaffordable for Japanese families with normal incomes, so that the purchasing power of a large part of the population fell drastically. The state itself was also heavily indebted, and could no longer even pay interest without imposing far-reaching restrictions on government spending.

In 1989, VAT was introduced in Japan for the first time through tax reform in order to increase the government's revenues. Domestic banks raised interest rates on their own to avoid excessive investment.

Japan's bubble economy burst. A ban on lending threw many Japanese companies into bankruptcy, which completed the vicious circle of the Japanese stock exchange. Real estate and land prices continued to fall, plunging Japan into a recession that can still be felt today.

Japan and Globalization

The recession is hanging like a heavy cloak around Japan's economy, which is trying to counteract it with new means. The Japanese Prime Minister, currently in his fourth term of office, is the most prominent. He launched the "Abenomics" program, which was designed to maximize government spending and help the Japanese economy grow.

To this end, investors from abroad were targeted in order to stimulate the Japanese market.

In 2012, the Nikkei Index rose sharply. However, this development did not continue. The principle of "Abenomics" also includes the constant printing of new money, which continues to devalue the yen. It is still unclear whether these measures will lead to long-term success for Japan's economy.

In general, it can be said that business relations between Japan and the rest of the world are not news. As early as the 1950s, many Japanese companies had set up branches in Europe to cover the local demand for products on the one hand and to expand service internationally on the other. However, the Japanese seldom find companies in Europe that are mainly engaged in the production of goods. The economic relationship between Japan and Europe can be regarded as capable of development. Japan's fundamental position in the world economy cannot be equated with the presence of Japanese companies in Europe.

Japan is anxious to close the economic gaps and position itself as a strong globalization partner. On 8 March 2018, for example, the country signed the transpacific free trade agreement CPTPP (Comprehensive and Progressive Trans-Pacific-Partnership), which came into being following the withdrawal of the USA from the previous trade agreement with the Pacific states. Eleven countries are involved, including Australia, Canada, Mexico, Chile and Peru. The tariffs within these trade routes are to be lowered and completely abolished. Such agreements promote globalization, as they facilitate the expansion of international companies in the world economic structure. A similar agreement is also being sought with the EU (JEFTA), which is highly controversial among the German population with regard to consumer protection, for example.

In addition, regular meetings of the various heads of state are held, such as the EU-Japan Summit, at which Japan's trade relations with the European Union were discussed in Brussels on 6 July 2018.

Fukushima

On 11.3.2011, Japan suffered a nuclear catastrophe again: Fukushima. Due to a devastating tsunami, the magnitude of which was clearly underestimated, combined with an earthquake of magnitude 9, the electricity in the nuclear power plant in Fukushima failed. The fuel rods could no longer be cooled sufficiently. This was followed by the dreaded core meltdown. Many volunteers helped with the clean-up work under life-threatening conditions, which made clear the loyalty of the Japanese for their own people.

For the second time in Japanese history, extensive residential areas were wiped out and a vast area of the country became uninhabitable. 18,000 people lost their lives or are missing. The rivers of the region have been contaminated to this day, as no suitable means of cleaning them have yet been found.

During this time, the government was clearly criticized for its information policy. Radioactive thresholds were glossed over, and people living near the disaster area were evacuated far too late. To this day, the actual effects of the radioactive radiation left behind by Fukushima are unclear. Many areas are still uninhabitable, and many people are waiting in container villages for possible repatriation or resettlement. The gradual release of the radioactively contaminated areas took place in March 2018. Among other things, Japan is again exporting fish from the Fukushima area to Thailand, as the limit values have not been exceeded for a longer period of time. But the people refuse to return to the old villages for fear of the consequences of the radiation. The trauma that the catastrophe left in people's minds is as present as ever. The areas currently remain largely uninhabited.

Japan's society today

Japan's society is characterized by an urban way of life, caused by the huge and constantly growing conurbation around the world metropolis Tokyo. About one-third of the entire Japanese population now lives in the Kanto region. Tokyo is also one of the most densely populated cities in the world. The average is around 340 people per square metre, and the trend is rising.

This development is underpinned by a steadily growing rural exodus: shops are closing in the countryside, ghost villages are emerging, as the job density is attracting more and more young people to the cities. Every effort is made to persuade the young population to stay. In the meantime, even real estate is simply given away.

Japan has few social aid systems to provide for non-working citizens, which further increases the pressure to perform in society. In the case of unemployment, for example, it is common for the state to pay out two-thirds of a person's previous salary as unemployment benefit over a period of three months to just under a year. In Japan, social assistance only exists for people who are unable to work (e.g. due to chronic illness) and employees who are not entitled to a pension.

Kaizen

The abundance of Japanese companies and firms is also reflected in the local culture. The principle of kaizen, originally a management concept from the nineties, is applied in all areas of life.

Kaizen fundamentally describes the continuous improvement of a work process. It is irrelevant whether perfection will ever be achieved. The goal is the gradual optimization of the end product. Japanese workers wish to transfer this attitude to their standard of living. Thus, the entrepreneurial philosophy spills over into everyday life. This can be seen in the respectful behaviour of the Japanese in public.

European companies also took advantage of this principle and still use it today for general quality management.

Demographic Change, Family and Lifestyle

As in Germany, the demographic change (Koreika) towards an older society is clearly present in Japan. The burden on social security is enormous in the long term. Japan, as well as Germany, is therefore urged to develop new systems to prevent poverty in old age.

The isolation of society is also a problem, which is drastically reflected in Japanese society. Fewer families and more singles are promoting demographic change. The family symbol is changing. Whereas in the past, it was mainly relatives who cared for their older family members. Today, there is a great demand for trained nurses.

Japan has many different lifestyles, some of which are viewed critically. The "Salary (wo)man" model stands out on the one hand. This woman or man, after graduating from university, is looking for work in various large companies. The subject in which the degree was obtained is of secondary importance here, since the graduates are trained in interdisciplinary flexibility. Every three years, a change of work location is planned. The company culture of the future employer is imparted to the career starters in various seminars.

The aim is to be promoted as far as possible. In the management positions, the workload is reduced and both the reputation and the salary increased considerably. In Japan, this linear lifestyle is considered to be particularly safe, but not very individual. Young people do not have the opportunity of creative time-out to get to know themselves, their wishes and interests. The consequences are increasing depression and loneliness, because with such a workload, there is little time for friends and family. This living apart leads to frequent divorces in the country, especially at retirement age, as the woman is financially secure with half of her husband's pension.

The strong work ethic, for which Japan is known above all internationally, gives way above all at present to an ever-greater desire of the young generation, towards more balance. The better compatibility of family and work is a goal, which the country should approach in the long run absolutely, in order to avoid a further sinking of the birth rate. Foreign companies could also take the place of Japanese companies due to a family-friendly working atmosphere. Many young Japanese seek employment in a company with less stringent working conditions to ensure their quality of life.

The planned curriculum vitae, which remains the ideal in Japan, was joined by a counter-movement at the end of the 1980s: The so-called Furita. This lifestyle is symbolized by constantly changing, temporary jobs that are often not lucratively remunerated. Working in retail or gastronomy is preferred by the Furita, as there is a high fluctuation of the workforce in these areas, and usually, no special training is necessary. The Furita have little opportunity to support a family financially. The result is an additional impoverishment of the young population of Japan, as the money is usually not even sufficient for their own needs.

Emancipation of women

Equality between men and women is difficult in Japan. Often, Japanese women are left with only simple jobs, such as "tea women" or secretaries. The majority of leadership positions are filled by men. It is very difficult to reconcile child and job in Japan, as part-time work is very unusual, and is not highly regarded. The Japanese government became aware of this social problem in the mid-1980s. The first law on equality between men and women came into force in 1985. However, this did not bear much fruit, and Japanese women still earn less than men. The decision between career and family is (as always) a problem that Japanese women inevitably have to deal with in the course of their lives. The acceptance of a working woman by the male side is limited. The classic distribution of roles is the social ideal, and is preferred by men as a family model. Women should have a good school leaving certificate, but after marriage, they should take care of their children and the household. Many Japanese women who want to break out of this outdated concept tend to have a relationship with a foreign man, as they are considered more tolerant and open in Japanese society.

A marriage arranged by the parents is not uncommon in Japan, as the children do not manage to find a suitable partner by the age of 30. The power of decision that parents still have over their children is indicative of the strict structures in which a young Japanese person grows up.

Suicide and the Japanese Society

Due to the isolation of society and the growing work pressure, especially on the young generation, the number of suicides in Japan is rising drastically. The documented numbers of other mental illnesses, such as burnout, are also increasing, especially among managers. Current studies by the WHO (World Health Organization) are alarming: suicide has become the number one cause of death among children and adolescents in Japan.

The incredible pressure to perform, which Japanese people already have to endure at school, has an early effect on the psyche. In secondary school, every fourth child can be diagnosed with depression. In addition, there is a very close approach to emotions and suffering, which is not openly addressed in Japan. The strong, sometimes violent hierarchies in Japanese schools are an open secret, and contribute to a toxic environment for children.

Migration

In the 20th century, Japan was considered a country of emigrants. Almost one million Japanese left their homeland at this time for economic reasons. The USA was a popular migration destination. After the Gentleman Agreement, which was founded in 1908 and regulated immigration to America, the Japanese travelled mainly to Brazil and Peru to build a new existence for themselves.

Migration is a topic that does not have a big platform in Japan. The demographic change initiated a rethinking. In the past, only qualified foreign specialists were allowed to enter the island state, and only for a limited period of time. Now, Japan is slowly beginning to open up and is facilitating a much simpler migration process. The proportion of foreigners in Japan is still low, and currently amounts to only about 1.7 percent of the total population. Many immigrants come from China, Brazil or the Philippines, and provide the urgently needed labour in the care and health sector. History has certainly shaped this sector, and in this context, the country's years of isolation in particular. Dealing with foreigners in Japan today is difficult, there is not much tolerance.

Despite the distanced attitude of the Japanese towards other population groups, stays abroad are obligatory, especially for students from a good home. Returning from such relatively short stays is easier than for those who grew up in another country. The many subliminally applied forms of social courtesy, rites and traditions often make integration very complicated. The government recognized the problem, and tried new regulations to facilitate the start for returning Japanese families by thinning out the bureaucracy, for example, for applying for a place at a Japanese university.

Mangas, Cosplay and Co.

Japan is characterized by a dichotomy. The rigid structures of society, often perceived from the outside as cool, are broken through by an expressive youth movement. The fascination for mangas, the Japanese comics, reaches as far as Germany. The associated costumes, which will be on display in Tokyo's districts, such as Akihabara as part of Cosplay, have become part of a new Japanese culture.

Young people identify with the various manga figures, which have their origins in Greek mythology, everyday life, science fiction, but also in the old Japanese empire. The possibilities are unlimited. This results in a sometimes-curious mixture of different clothing forms, which suggests certain openness towards other cultures and traditions.

As a draughtsman of Japanese comics, you can sometimes build up a considerable fortune. The profession is highly regarded in Japan, not least because the painting technique has its origin in the traditional woodcuts, and picture rolls of that time. Through the sale of her comics and additional merchandising, such as action figures, video games, DVDs and music, artists such as Naoko Takeushi (Sailor Moon, 1992) and Akira Toryiama (Dragonball, 1984) made millions.

The fans of such a scene culture call themselves "Otaku". This passion can go to extremes and produce experts in various fields.

With the help of this colourful, cheerful and creative movement, the Japanese have managed to relativize their image of the ever-working suits in international society. For many Western readers, mangas and animes (comic-strip films often based on mangas) offer a window on Japanese culture that they would otherwise not have been interested in. The result is a growing interest in the western world in the Japanese way of life.

Japan and North Korea

As the critical relationship between the USA and North Korea intensified, the general security situation in Asia, Japan discussed possible investments in the country's military defence in 2017. Until now, the state has been anxious to maintain its pacifist, defensive stance so as not to violate its own constitution. However, this could change with the fourth term of the incumbent prime minister. More room for manoeuvre for the Japanese military is just one of many demands made by Abes that will determine how North Korea is treated in the future.

So that Japan can confidently oppose North Korea's nuclear policy, Shinzo Abe intends to expand cooperation with major powers such as China, the USA and Russia. The main objective is to secure peace in the Asian region with the help of diplomatic negotiations. The Japanese are very critical of the unpredictable North Korean head of government.

End

This introduction should summarize the essential points of Japanese history and give a first insight. It is impossible to fully grasp all the factors that may be relevant to Japanese history.

Japan's deep connection with its history and the pride that unites the Japanese people has come to the fore. From antiquity to the time of the shoguns and emperors, to modern times, the island state absorbed many different influences and traditions, be it through religions such as Shintoism or Buddhism, as well as the influential family clans of the Middle Ages to the present day. It is interesting to note that these family power structures have remained in a modern way until modern times, if one looks at the Zaibatsu, which have their origins in the clans of the Japanese late Middle Ages.

Despite many conflicts within the country, a unified, cohesive society developed, which is currently experiencing a peaceful era without excessive conflicts. The pacifist ideas, as part of the constitution, distinguish today's Japan from many other superpowers.

Today's Japan is not only characterized by its loyalty to its historical tradition. The Japanese youth brings a breath of fresh air into the conservative social structures. Their expressive pop culture is known all over the world, and is accompanied by a great fascination, be it through cosplay, manga or karaoke. Throughout the world, Japan's scene culture has gained sympathy and interest among young people. The export of traditional food, such as sushi, also offers a window to the once so isolated Asian world. Japan is becoming increasingly popular with tourists.

Many different factors make Japan the country it is today: full of contrasts, economically strong and with great potential. Despite the great influence of China and Korea, the island state has managed to build its own identity and stand out from the rest of Asia.

The speed with which Japan developed into an economic power made the courage to change within the country clear. The innovations, especially in the field of technology, are highly regarded in the international markets. Japan is a state authority with a unique selling point in world history. High medical standards and comparatively good average salaries make Japan an attractive home for young professionals.

It remains to be seen whether Prime Minister Shinzo Abe's policy can bring Japan out of the recession. However, with the growing popularity of the Japanese towards the West and its way of life, there is definitely a great tendency towards globalization. The economy also seems to be recovering: the appreciation of the yen in 2018 is a widespread forecast among financial experts. Japanese companies are also recording far-reaching successes, and are currently keeping the Nikkei index on a good course. Japan could be in the process of overtaking China in its rapid expansion.

Demographic change is currently the country's most threatening problem. The mortality rate continues to exceed the birth rate. If this does not change, the Japanese population could shrink drastically within the next few decades. With a large number of senior citizens compared to children, the Japanese can be described as a population group threatened with extinction. Here, it is important that ways and means are created to expand the infrastructure for families, and also to enable working women to better reconcile childhood and work. A growing openness towards migration and the refugee crisis can help Japan to have more promising prospects for the future. A more open approach to mental illness should also be on the agenda if the general health of the Japanese population is to be improved on a sustainable basis.

How the situation in Asia will develop with regard to North Korea is still unclear. Japan is anxious to represent a strong military authority on the continent in order to defend the lasting peace. For the West, such a consolidated alliance would be beneficial in terms of the uncertainty of North Korean policy.

The relationship with the US is an important future factor for Japan and world politics. Donald Trump and Shinzo Abe agreed at their meeting in Washington in early 2017. The Prime Minister's conciliatory attitude towards the controversial US President can be seen as an intelligent move in the trade relationship between Japan and the US. Abe announced his intention to invest even more in the US, and to stand up with Trump for the security of the Pacific. It is not yet clear how the ideas of the heads of state will ultimately affect the communities of states.

The excursion into the history of Japan will help us to better understand the culture and customs of the Asian island state. The Japanese people have survived many crises, and have maintained a certain serenity about the current problems in world politics. The initially diffuse power relations have led to a democratically founded form of government without external control. This makes Japan an interesting model of state development for historians and political researchers.

Viktoria Niebuhr

Legal notice and imprint

The work including all contents is protected by copyright. Reprinting or reproduction, in whole or in part, as well as storage, processing, reproduction and distribution with the aid of electronic systems, in whole or in part, is prohibited without the written permission of the author. All translation rights reserved.

The contents of this book have been researched from recognized sources and checked with great care. Nevertheless, the author does not assume any liability for the topicality, correctness and completeness of the information provided.

Liability claims against the author, which refer to damages of health, material or ideal nature, which were caused by use or misuse of the presented information and/or by the use of incorrect and incomplete information, are in principle, impossible.

This book is no substitute for medical or professional advice and care.